The Dedalus Press

THE OLD WOMEN OF MAGIONE

Ciaran O'Driscoll

The Old Women Of Magione

CIARAN O'DRISCOLL

The Dedalus Press
24 The Heath, Cypress Downs, Dublin 6W. Ireland

ISBN 1 901233 08 1 (paper) The Dedalus Press
ISBN 1 901233 09 X (bound) The Dedalus Press

Cover design by David Lilburn

Acknowledgments:
Some of these poems have previously appeared in *Cyphers, The Irish Times, Loose Ends (BBC Radio 4), Off the Shelf (RTE Radio 1), The Poetry Ireland Review, Potpourri (USA)*.

Thanks to the Cultural Relations Committee of the Dept. of Foreign Affairs, Dublin, for grants to assist participation in the Tratti Folk Festival, Faenza, 1995, and the Festival Franco-Anglais de Poésie, Paris 1997. And to 'Immagini d'Irlanda in Umbria' for facilitating participation in the festival of that name, Perugia 1994.

Special thanks to Paul Cahill and Fernando Trilli for their friendship and generosity in making possible my year's stay in Umbria with my family, also to their friends who became our friends, and to the many others in the town of Magione and its environs who made us feel more than welcome.

sad nets / the sea's rustling girdle in 'Mixed Salad' are images from Pablo Neruda's 'Twenty Love Poems & a Song of Despair'.

Dedalus Books are represented and distributed in the U.K. and Europe by *Password*, 2-4 Little Peter St., Manchester M15 4PS. In the USA and Canada by *Dufour*, PO Box 7, Chester Springs, Pennsylvania 19425.

Printed in Ireland by Colour Books Ltd.

The Dedalus Press receives financial assistance from An Chomhairle Ealaíon, The Arts Council, Ireland.

for Margaret and Conor

CONTENTS

Ora di Partire

You have reached a halfway house,
and you're halfway where you want to be
and halfway not, and friends
whose grasp of love was tenuous
are no longer around,
and day follows day and you know
that things have changed but hardly dare
to admit it, *their friendship was sloth,*
they were drinking you into their death
until the taste of whatever life
remained in you no longer pleased
their palates, and they spat you out,
and you've landed on the ground
in front of this halfway house,
which is really the carriage of a train
in the dullness of a pre-dawn station.

And you know the stance of a waiting train
in the stubbled light of dawn,
the rest of wheels provisional
below the level of the platform,
and not to be deceived by rest
you know the cues, the small subliminal
quickenings towards the moment;
better than you know the ice
of faces or the skill of melting ice.

And sometimes still a molecule or two
of yours can bond in the endless chain
of the laughter of your son,
and times will come when you are indisposed
to attend the annual festival
when cherry blossom leaps its prison wall,
but *Nothing happens in these trenches*
say the features in their permafrost,
Go now and don't come back unless
to bring us home the secret . . .

And you must enter again
the comforting musty embrace
of a carriage in an almost empty train.

A Former Franciscan

A Former Franciscan Visits Assisi

(1)

Begin on the level, on the Plain
of Umbria, the road winding
up towards the fortress-like Basilica
on the slopes of Monte Subasio.

Begin where it all began,
here, with the literal interpretation,
a matter of stone and mortar,
and the bare hands of a saint
repairing a tiny chapel
now dwarfed in the pillared interior
of Santa Maria degli Angeli.

Begin by asking what,
if anything, went wrong
that such towering structures should
entomb a simple church, enshrine
our memory of a humble man.
A case, perhaps, of the essential thing
that's always lost in the translation,
greatness of spirit rendered by
a monument's enormity?

And the best we can do is erect
monuments wherever
the spirit passed on its way,
and build museums where the clay
once fired in a shape of uncommon love
fell to pieces and rests.

(2)

On a blistering day in Rome
we walked the marches
of piazze, fora, churches
that were temples once, and churches
that from the beginning had been churches;
and I was the one in five
reluctant to receive
that peripatetic visual
education, the one who shrank
from marvelling at mosaics
because it entailed looking at saints,
and recoiled from a rococo pulpit
carved in dark wood because it brought
a distasteful memory to light
of a time I led the rosary
from a similar height.
Unhappy in my brown habit,
in guilty love with a girl of twenty,
I heard a voice in my inner
ear as I doled out
those indulgence-laden decades,
a voice I thought at best
was that of Martin Luther's ghost,
or, at worst, the voice of the Devil,
which said *By partaking in this*
charade of pious unctiousness
you are being untrue to yourself
and your deepest convictions –

a voice I've since acknowledged as my own.

(3)

And now at the open gate
of the Portiuncula, I hesitate
as usual, but sense
suddenly a difference :
that here the unadorned truth
is at the centre of the show;
an unpretentious holy place
remaining in the heart
of a mausoleum of religious art.

And likewise in Assisi,
all the way to and through
the lower and upper Basilicas,
through narrow medieval streets
up to the old Piazza
where Minerva's christened temple
still rests on Corinthian columns,
something unobtrusive, pure
and inexpressible is in the air,

and in their streetside booths,
even the hawkers of mementoes,
taking a page from the Poverello's book,
are selling their trinkets cheap.

(4)

Where is the handle to grip
the empirical reality
of this phantom of a former self
and crank it into poetry?

And what kind of poetry machine
could be animated, driven
by this supererogatory ghost,
when even Giotto and the best
of thirteenth-century engineers
have failed their driving test?

Better to be this old woman
clinging to a grid of St Francis' tomb
in an anguish of everyday despair,
as I clung once to unanswered prayer
on a kneeler in the dark
of a tiny oratory
at the end of the open ward
in a psychiatric hospital,
a chaplain fallen into the fosse
of love with a student nurse
when the game was up for the liberals
and the posse of hard-riding country clergy
thundered with a vengeance
to head off at the next pass
the reforms of Pope John XXIII;

better to cling thus, than daily
to stare at the mechanical reality
society has become, to be

a cog in a meaningless machine
cranking from sleep to routine :
because prayer at the very least
is an infusion of hope
that some day things will change,
that some day word and world
will be reconciled,

even for an old woman at the grave's
edge, and all who grapple
with the inexpressible.

(5)

Back home, the screen of my word processor
questions the ghost of Assisi's
most famous confessor;
as the imprint of our short sojourn
in Umbria fades, an inquisitor
scans the electronic page
looking for something concrete
to which he can relate;

and we know in this sceptical day and age
that Augustine's *memoria*
(self-presence) is conditional
on the functioning of the brain cell,

we are aware of Alzheimer's
and similar degenerative diseases,
consciousness-raising substances,
philosophers propose identity
of mind and body,
and the adage to the effect
that there's no cure for growing old
has assumed a brutal finality
that Francis praising Sister Death
would find – to understate –
quite uncongenial.

The gates of Paradise are closed,
and self-presence erodes
as the brain ages, the memory
fragments and plays tricks,
and an octogenarian sits,
sallow and shrinking in his clothes,
falling into a doze
and waking paranoia-eyed,
on the same seat all day,
this lack of mind-body identity
that was my father once.

(6)

I can speak quite concretely, meaningfully,
of inter-generational hostility,
having lost my father a long time before
he began to lose himself.
And everything I've done
from the age of twenty –
entering and leaving the church,
becoming an armchair Marxist radical,
then abandoning a Ph. D
on Political Justice to search
for the elusive approval
of the world of English Lit.
(while my verses often castigated it) –
has perhaps been a symbolic chase
after sonship fallen from grace,
and re-enactment of the primal split.

A patriarchal wall of unbreakable glass
has kept my father from me to the last,
and watching him through it now
I am as impotent emotionally
as he is impotent in every way
to talk of reconciliation.

Better to change the world, because
it made my father what he was.

(7)

First there was one God,
and then there was none.

And when there was a God,
there were miraculous signs.
If the thought of praying entered his head,
and the clock struck the hour
immediately after, a young novice
fell on his knees before
the crucifix in his cubicle.

These days I might as well
be praying to a spanner
or monkey wrench for deliverance from
the quotidian grind's boredom,
its non-eventuality.
If he cannot abide in the fraternity,
let him go and do penance in the world –
a world whose only sign
is billboard or neon,
a vacuous jingle on the radio;
and at the end of the perilous journey
the adman's TV travesty
of myth : the tree of Adam bearing fruit
in little plastic tubs of yoghurt.

Sometimes, admittedly, the world
can still of a sudden
assume a resonance beyond
the one-dimensional, as the sun
sometimes breaks through the Irish summer's

ample blanket of cloud-cover.
And sometimes even in the rain
there comes a moment when
the bird on a neighbouring roof
is an ancient symbol or hieroglyph
in the book of the riddle's meaning.

And this is poetry, when the bird
preaches to you, and you respond
by preaching strictly for the birds.

(8)

And there are those who say
the saint moved towards his death
burdened by compromise imposed
on the freedom he wished to bequeath
his followers, and often grieved
at Rome's relentless pressure
to put it down in black and white,
with copious footnotes to meet
every eventuality conceived
in the legalistic heads
of clerics more concerned
with drawing boundaries round
experience than experiencing; so

the perpetual struggle between
those who make ever more
fastidious maps of the known,
and those who venture beyond
the maps' margins
to become explorers, bandits,
revolutionaries, heretics, pirates,
great sinners or great saints,
or even both in one lifetime,
in that valley obscured by clouds
where burnt-out poets end their days
as gun-runners, and drug-pushers
turn humanitarian prodigies.

(9)

And when I was leaving them,
the Franciscans handed me
a map of my future
where every road that failed
to return me to the friary
within a year was marked
either *To Territories
Unknown* or *Cul de Sac.*
And there was a friar I knew
who for years had parodied
the circular journey approved
by ecclesiastical cartography,

leaving and coming back,
and leaving and coming back,
swinging like a pendulum
between the polarities
of security and freedom;
who may be vacillating still
for all I know, in real life,
as I do still in dream,
where I have often found myself
robed in a brown Franciscan habit
although I wanted to profess
among new friends new worldliness,
or saying to a former
spiritual director
It's difficult for me to stay
now that I have a wife and son.
In my case the mind's oscillation
seems to be slowing down at last
to the middle point of rest.
But it has taken twenty years,
charting singlehandedly
the valleys of love and lust,
the mountains of ambition,
the boglands of deceit,
the cities of hope, despair and rage,
the desert of frustration,
to have, if only for a while,
a firm road beneath my feet.

(10)

And have I not heard those stories
about ex-priests gone astray,
discovered *in extremis*
fallen from the carriages
of goods trains at spaghetti junctions,
and their incoherent accounts
of failed careers and broken marriages?
Have I not often heard
about those defrocked fugitives
from the law or their ruined lives,
clutching bottles of tawny port
in the squalor of back streets,
their last misdirected swigs
a feeble foray at the dregs,
and their scarcely audible dying words
I should never have left?
And while I might suspect
that these were but examples
of the kinds of myths which protect
believers from self-doubt
(because in is in and out
must be out in the cold
for an institution growing old
unable to tell its resistance
to change from the pursuit
of its original intentions),
I was nonetheless susceptible,
and after each new failure
in the world of work and love,
myself took to the bottle
in order to obliterate

the sense of hostile fate
that oppressed me for weeks,
believing the Manichean God
from whom I fled
had created day and night
with no gradations of twilight,
and I was some kind of leper
who had not been embraced
by heaven or by earth,
with scarcely the right to exist.

(11)

Where, then, was the period
of debriefing I badly needed
after years of abnegation,
where the assertiveness training
a half-ways benevolent body
might have provided any
long-serving but disenchanted member
it had shaped to a passivity
at odds with shipping out
on seas of *laissez-faire* and anarchy?

Where was that soft fading of light,
when I needed it, between the bright
certainty of an overall purpose
and the haphazard darkness
where no purpose exists
outside what the individual
can shape by putting his own dent
on the warring elements?

(12)

You can take the monk out of the cloister
but it needs a lot longer
to take the cloister out of the monk.

And there have been so many
events and places where
you were bodily present
but essentially absent
since you left the cloister;
so many things you can't remember –
what certain people looked like,
in what surroundings did
certain conversations
occur; blackouts caused
not by alcohol as much
as the damage done by God
when he took you over and made
you absent from yourself,
and you couldn't shake him off,
which meant you weren't really *there*,
for hours on end, wherever you were,
and your five senses so
weakened and confused
by their term in custody, so used
to their mufflers and their hoods,
remained shut off from the world.

And desire, grown enormous
in its absolute of absence,
refused to settle for anything less
than the absolute of sex;

and the totality of touch
in the possession of another's
body was the only thing
that could make your senses sing.

(13)

And I wonder how many like me
there are who disappear
into that non-identity,
the Church's *desaparecidos* who
go missing without warning from themselves,
suddenly in the middle
of a family meal,
or at a crucial interview,
causing their loved ones distress
or egregiously failing to impress
at the strategic moment
because they have fallen back
over the void's unmapped edge?

(14)

Take a last look
at the floodlit facade,
its enormous rose window
guarded by griffons.

Sunset blackens the plain
below, and the winding road
is a necklace of lights.
The alternating pink and white
of the limestone facings
has ceded to an orange pallor,
and the doors are shut,
the Basilica is closed.
And underneath all
are the arched buttresses
of silence, fastening reality
to its slippery rock,
and above is the silence of the sky
crossed by a shred of cloud.
And here, a pinprick
somewhere between the foundations
and the dome of the universe,
insignificant, hardly
daring to breathe, are you.
And yet you have survived
and are surviving; say goodbye
to the haunting illusion
that led you nowhere, the rose
of the world that might be raised
to the power of infinity.
You have other matters to attend,
different responsibilities.

Finish your grieving now
for what you were and might have been
under the arch where the twin
portals are closed as gates
of the earthly paradise were
to the old age of your father.
Begin again as the saint began,
not with a disembodied notion
of universal brotherhood
but with a literal interpretation
of loving in the here-
and-now of brick and mortar.

You who have been reborn in blood
through husbandry and parenthood.

The Sleep-Journey

Between your eyelashes and eyebrows
your four-year-old skin is rose and violet;
your face is calm as the lake's surface,
a continuance in changing light.
In this journey we have to undertake,
yours is the fastest mode of transport:
under closed eyelids
a hurtling through tunnels of friendly space.
When I look at you, son, I think of the lake,
I think of the mountain, of
the cornucopia of the hills,
I think of the land's image of infinity;
and of the many connections we must make,
the train, the plane, the car, the waiting
in the indifference of terminals;
I think of de Chirico's *Anguish of Departure*,
and what the eyes of children wake to
in transit camps and refugee ships;
what we put into the eyes of children.
But you, as yet among the spared,
will open eyes whose infinity
has not been staked out and divided up
among the factions of desolation;
there are eyes to meet yours that are not those
of clinical carers or worse; your sleep is not
escape from sorrow but a running leap
from one good day to the next, the sleep
of the mountain, of the surface of the lake,
the sleep of the land's largesse. You are
fragile and loved as your
uncertain gesture in this photograph,
holding wild flowers to the lip
of an earthenware jug.

The Old Women of Magione

Headgear

We're on our way to Italy,
to live a year before life passes by,
and I've jettisoned my Guinness cap
along a mountain road not on the map.

Living in hope has proved a lie;
the less things change, the more
they stay the same : get an eye
full of the Alps before you die.

Bask in the sun before you croak.
When sun came out, the traveller shed his cloak,
what storm wanted him to do,
but when the cold wind blew

he wrapped it closer round.
I threw my Guinness cap to ground
on an unmapped road and let it lie
amid majestic scenery.

Fill me another and another jug
of Southern wine till bankers pull the plug;
and here's to grazing in rich grass,
a year away from the middle class.

I've gained a zest for life; I'll do without
my headgear advertising Irish stout.

Basil

(for the Gemini)

When the first had driven us to the house from Chiusi station, the second appeared at the door of our apartment carrying a dish of scrambled eggs and zucchini flavoured with the sweet cloying herb around which my memories cluster.

On the table just inside the door, by the window looking out on the compound where they kept geese and Tibetan goats and hens, on the edge of the self-seeding oakwoods, there was already a two-litre plastic water-bottle filled with home-made wine, and a torta of welcome.

As I write, the scent of it clings to my fingers. There was a small garden where it grew between tomatoes and auber-gines. That year we made no sugo or pastasciutta, we simply spread it on sliced tomatoes or imitating our first meal in Umbria used it to flavour scrambled eggs.

It is synonymous in my memory with the sun and heat of late June and early July, its perfume mingles with the glitter of Lago Trasimeno and the taste of birra alla spina at the beach between Toricella and Monte del Lago, with the impressionist ambience of Pub Franci in Magione, with Carlo Lillini's multicoloured waistcoats.

That scent and the dusty white roads of La Goga, and the sun beating down as we climbed a hill in the late morning, gasping past rows of inscrutable olive trees.

That delicate herb and the unyielding olive trees, their small bitter fruit, their small dark green and silver leaves, foliage that changes colour, blanches and darkens with light and weather. On hillsides they stand impermeable as rows of apostles and church fathers on façades of cathedrals, each one twisted into its own peculiar shape of virtue and all of them tough and unbending as the will of a saint.

But the other is delicate and easily wilted, its power in the sweetness that teases some lost corner of memory, some dim recess of existence. Its strength is its weakness, the fragility of new life that cannot come out of its potency, that you think it's better to leave alone, leave be in its half existence because there's enough of the impermeability of apostles, the density of olive trees and the heat of the midday sun which keeps you in the cool shelter of your terracotta-tiled apartment.

And so you leave it to its intangible associations, because it's better that way, because in that way tangible memories can cluster round an untouchable source, a bright green evanescence in the void of summer, like the cuckoo's voice creating the depths of the surrounding woods.

It's better that way because otherwise you'll want to die when your lips remain dumb for so long and the acrid sweetness on your fingers creates a vague shaft of green light in your mind becoming an even vaguer corridor leading nowhere.

Better to think the other way. It wasn't that you allowed this plant into your life; it has chosen you to peer into a disappearing essence as you sit surrounded by days of sunshine and the inexhaustible cathedrals of Italy, and the earth tilled to infinity and the endurance of the olives and hillsides faintly striped, and evening sun chroming the lake and the islands merging into one another and re-emerging, and pastel archers dancing like prime donne round a bored Saint Sebastian in Panicale, and life, like some strange species of erect animal, advancing out of holes in the stonework onto the dusty piazza of late afternoon.

It's all very beautiful and too much, its essence like the scent that overpowers you tearing the spray from the plant, and the next moment when you ask *But what is it?* there's no reply, only the voice of the cuckoo or úpupa travelling through light years of stillness.

And you need a beer down at the lake to get you back on a windsurfer's even keel, you need to be confronted eyeball to watch pocket by Carlo Lillini's multicoloured waistcoat as he takes your order for a pizza and a litre of frizzante.

And you need to get good and drunk and set all the dogs barking in La Goga on the way home, howling like you under the clear night sky.

And you navigate the dirt tracks between the tobacco fields by the stars on your way to the sleep that lies behind that teasing scent of morning.

Travelling from Torino, 22 March 1995

1.

My father was famous for five days
a few weeks after his death;
a gale that lashed the coast of Clare
and ploughed the sea to acres of froth,
he boomed around our Easter Holiday
cottage, keeping us in
as he often did in life, cracking
the whip of his stormy authority;
and every venture into the open
was an act of rebellion
that summoned its courage from
the blistering summers of my teens.

A dark figure in front of the sun
as it set alongside the parish church,
he'd shout down the street in Irish
A Chiaráin tar anseo as I returned
rising from the hollow of the lower town
onto the plateau of the market square,
home from a day of idleness
on the river bank, with jokes and talk of sex,
and sometimes my mouth burned
with the tangible memory of a kiss,
but *A Chiaráin tar anseo* dispelled
it all and brought me back to ground,
suddenly embarrassed and furious
at his voice's patriarchal boom
in the tongue of dead patriots
and the school curriculum.

2.

One night as I pushed against the wind
to close the door of the car,
the five-day gale
made away with my new felt hat;
I saw it leap into the dark
above the headlights, then
suddenly grounded spin
round a corner like a runaway wheel.
An old anger drove me to search
uselessly with a feeble torch,
not to be deprived by him again
of anything that expressed
my tenuous identity,
although my friends were sure the sea
had claimed it almost as soon
as it left my head,
and once I shouted *Easy, Dad!*
to the sky and the hidden moon
to the elements possessed.
And I was angry that the dead
would not lie down with their
unfinished business. The next day
my hat was found by weekend neighbours,
but not the same, the grey
was mottled with patches of rust,
and later, when the band burst,
the shape was lost for good.
Here in Italy, short of money,
I wore it on winter walks
till, rain-drenched once more
in a February downpour,

at last I let it go
as I am inclined to do
with headgear and identities; I threw
it to rot on the balcony
and the sleeping dogs that lie
on anything soft that's left out there
flattened and covered it with hair.

3.

This morning in Torino,
waking in the *Hotel Bologna*,
I half-expected to see
my father sitting at the end of the bed,
a troubled shade haunting me
on his first aniversary,
but opened my eyes instead
to an emptiness full of distance
under the white arc, the sweep
of the rough-cut mountains,
in a room swept utterly clean
of everything but morning light,
and I spoke into the distance :

Dad, you're not with me any more,
you don't talk to me any more,
we were never really together
in your lifetime, never really spoke.
And I can't say that I miss
you, but at least I can say this :
more than your presence did, today
your absence has begun to speak.

4.

Watching the scene from a speeding train
in Piemonte now, I view
all that with equanimity.
A year is a long time, and today
my father has been dead a year,
and looking at the mountains
I think of my son, his eyes
turning deeper blue when he cries,
the sudden copious tears
trickling down to his chin
or running into his mouth's corners,
their unpredictable trajectories
like rain on glass, his cheeks
as wet as windows.
I think of my son and swear I'll bring
him here to the mountains' foot
to see these Alpine peaks
on some future anniversary;

a day like this in spring
when Italy is bathed in sunlight.

Ercolano

I think of the name of Ercolano
as I wait for the bus to the volcano
in the cramped and dusty square
below the Circumvesuviana,
wondering what I'm doing here,
and a taxi driver from Positano
tries to convince me his costly fare
offers much more than does the *pulmino*.

What I feel when I think of Ercolano
is fear of a sleeping volcano
that poured down rivers of ash and lava
and hot lapilli on Herculaneum
and Pompei, making a mausoleum
of life's traffic one afternoon
while sunlight tinkled on the grand piano
of the Mediterranean.

What I hear in the name of Ercolano
is the impatient shuffling of our feet
on a piazza of dusty concrete,
the rock of money in the *piano piano*
persistence of the taxi driver,
market's cry and motor's revving rather
than sweetness of tenor or soprano;
traffic of life under the volcano.

Carp

(for John Coughlan and Olive Beecher)

We were between the pasta and the *secundo piatto*, sitting at an open-air table across the street from the hotel, on an island in the middle of a lake, drinking white wine on a day of rolling clouds and sunlight, the white linen tablecloth sprinkled by sporadic raindrops.

We were waiting for the carp. In the somewhat unnerving quiet of the season before the season, we were the only visible diners. A trickle of explorers passed on their way to the island paths, the ruined castello and chapel, the church with its gory frescoes and the hermitage where St Francis had fasted for forty days.

We had come because we heard about the carp. It was the region's greatest delicacy, they said, and no one cooked it better than in this island restaurant. *Carpa Regina in Porchetta*, they said; incisions were made and filled with fennel, garlic and the lard of suckling pig, the gaps were bushed with sprigs of rosemary, and it was grilled on a spit.

We drank and the talk fell flat as we waited. I took to taking in my surroundings, the intractrable antiquity of walls and doors, the garish pink fishing nets spread out on both sides of the brick pavement which is the island's only street.

Someone was voicing the opinion that this delay between courses was a management ploy to increase our consumption of wine, when a small commotion nearby distracted us from rancour.

A grim little porcession was passing in front of us. A tall man wearing a suit led the way, turning frequently to talk and gesture at another, smaller and dressed in fisherman's gear and waders.

The smaller man was the juggler in this truncated circus parade, balancing a large quivering fish precariously on the spike of a gaff. The tall man was now motioning him towards steps which led up to a side door of the hotel.

Suddenly the sun broke from behind the rolling clouds and brightened the scales of the fish, gilding its lozenged skin.

Vision

The leaves will not alter their cast
however hard you stare;
they are set as a face on a Roman tomb,
and a face they are.

No matter how long you gaze
or from how many perspectives,
moving your chair around
the balcony, that face-in-leaves

does not revert to foliage.
And although you feel in your bones
the dripping of wet branches,
the multitudinous veins

of water crossing leaves,
dropping from those above to those
below, to rivulets and stream,
what you see down there is a face.

Read nothing into this head
garlanded with the ascending wood;
for the past few weeks you have
been drinking more than you should.

Úpupa

Úpupa, úpupa, úpupa,
say the gentlemen in black and white tails
who have just arrived from Africa.

Úpupa, úpupa, úpupa.
The days are sunning out
in Umbria, and the *stranieri*
enrolling in bigger numbers
for language courses in Perugia.

Úpupa, úpupa, úpupa,
says the sartorially flamboyant
seasonal migrant
with fancy crest and fastidious bill,
while the tree by my window is shrill
with the lingo of tits and sparrows.

Úpupa, úpupa, úpupa.
The year begins its downhill roll,
fresco-viewing in cathedrals
impeded by clustering groups
of teenagers on school-
tours straining at the leash.

Úpupa, úpupa, úpupa.
Out in the lush
of the fields, hills and woods,
everything stops but growth.
Tractors unharnessed after
endless ploughing, vine-buds
sprouting untended on trellises.

Úpupa, úpupa, úpupa,
while the cuckoo has the sonorous edge,
borrowing resonance from timber
for the unmatched timbre
of life's two-syllable compendium,
the fullness and finality of it all.

But *úpupa, úpupa, úpupa,* as a call,
is somehow simultaneously
closer and more distant,
coming from a less audible
but greater Nowhere,
whose matter is woven of three syllables,
softer but going further.

Something

There was something I was trying to put my finger on all
that summer, you know what I'm like when I get my teeth
into something, only this was something you couldn't get
your teeth into, I couldn't even put my finger on it, not even
after a few pints, and you know what I'm like after a few
pints, not that you could get a pint over there without it
costing an arm and a leg, but even after a bottle of Orvieto
or two I couldn't get a handle on it, we'd sit on the balcony
into the small hours watching moths bouncing round the
light, we'd take the world apart and put it back together
again, but for me there was always something missing, I
couldn't find it dismantling the scheme of things nor would
it click into place when I reassembled the elements more to
my liking, I'd have been as well employed draining the lake
as a new way of fishing for carp or ironing the creases out
of the Appenines.

Don't get me wrong, I was having a good time of it, down
at the beach every day, sitting in the same place, on the
concrete edge between the sand and the grass, equidistant
between the bar and the water, the sun beating its numbing
pleasure into my brain as I looked at the lake and the olive
groves on the hills beyond, the sailboards skimming the
waves or the white sails of a yacht disappearing behind an
island, and all around me the multiple bella figura of solar
dedication, the resolution of all values into *bronze, bronzer
and bronzest*, the endless conjugation of self-reflexive verbs
and the shaded eyes of would-be directors rehashing their
revisions of *La Dolce Vita* out of the leavings of their momen-
tary lusts.

That's how it was, something always escaping, though I often enviously imagined others had a hold of it and didn't know they had, some gift or other you'd become aware of only when you lost it, a kind of blessedness there was no way of keeping if it was destined to desert you, that you couldn't intend about like getting married or buying a car or going out for the evening or writing a book, something you couldn't promise never to let go of because if you began to think like that it was already on the way out, already slipping away.

What could I do only look, not that I minded just looking, I saw everything from a distance, sometimes admittedly I made a gesture towards working off the lardo grasso in the swim or playing tennis with my wife or showing my son some fancy footwork, but mostly I sat on the concrete edge between the water and the grass, taking everything in, composing my picture, until I became part of the lakeside ambience, wasps and beached driftwood, pedal boats and waving flags, the annual snowfall of poplar seeds, volleyball courts and swings and roundabouts, burnt middle-aged foreigners and old wistful Englishmen in khaki looking like displaced desert-campaign commanders.

And when I talked about it, I often suspected that those listening to me thought I was talking about something else, because I had names for it, one night one name and another night another, and the names meant something specific and something different each night, of course I had to use names or I couldn't talk at all, but it slipped in and out between the names, as if you could call it firefly one night and children the next and fresco the night after, and so everyone thought

48

I was holding forth on entomology or education or medieval art, and in a way I was, but in another way I wasn't but trying instead to talk about something so simple it didn't have a name, so difficult it couldn't be expressed.

And there you have it, every day the trip from the car under the trees to the place in the sun between the bar and the water, heat and light eventually sapped the life out of whatever bothered me until it paled away, a fisherman by the lake's edge becoming a transparent wavecrossed image of himself, or the flickering of invisible timetables on the silversides of poplar leaves; as if an Etruscan bar code crossing the lazer at a checkout till had set an infinite series of ciphers in motion.

Quality Fish

In the country of powder-paint-yellow
dry-as-dust dog-eared sunflowers,
up there behind those cypresses,
an Englishman has cornered more
than his share of the summer water supply,
and basks in the shade of trees all day
beside the amethyst surface
of his swimming pool, the jewel
of a secret British colony
buried in the woods like a truffle.
Hidden from the eyes of men on tractors
whose roar is a distant murmur in his ears,
he's a retired fishmonger
from somewhere up North –
And it's three score and ten boys and men
were lost from Grimsby Town –
and he tells me he used to deal
in Quality Fish, but Thatcher let him down.
All day he stays in the shade,
one patch of foreign soil
forever England. While
the rasping stillness rages
towards forty degrees,
and the only noonday idea
of man and beast is to survive,
above all not to move,
he rises now and then
to check the level of the pool
and settles back again
into his one green thought,
to make this sylvan hideaway

in the baked earth of landlocked Umbria
an agritourist stop
on the British Foreign Holiday Map.
But sometimes in the gin-
and-tonic flavoured aquamarine
depths of his memory,
rarer and rarer admittedly,
there may still float into view
a Quality Fish, lonely and lost,
from waters off the English coast,
From Yarmouth up to Scarborough . . .

Decisions

I hear my son's bicycle still
the ticking of its chain,
although I no longer see him
since he veered into a dusty lane,
pedalling backside raised head down
as if he couldn't extend
the six years of his life
except by covering ground.

The leaning water-jets
in nearby fields are shaking veils
of spray on thirsty corn,
olive groves in the wooded hills
are coats-of-arms, family shields;
and on a tower above the town,
steel of neglected scaffolding
eats into ancient stone.

A few more minutes' walking
and I have reached the turn
where my cyclist re-appears,
dismounted, crestfallen,
wheeling the small machine
that is suddenly an impediment
back towards me, now he wants
to follow some other bent.

And the question that bothers me is
Should I let him have his head
or remind him of our pact,
to cycle the whole way or not
at all? Decisions too may eat
into the possible future,
like steel tubes into what
they were erected to restore.

Alfredo

Still young and thin, my grandfather stands in the ploughed
    field,
even in summer he rarely unbuttons
the chequered shirt he wears over his woollen vest.
Matted with dust and sun when the sourness of virgin wine
catches his throat and pearls his forehead with sweat,
facing the valley he sniffs the sudden August rain
about to beat down on the donkey's pack-saddle,
on his quenched cigar, on his cap askew, on steaming
    furrows.
Sometimes my grandfather stops in mid-stride without
    speaking,
looks far away over the mountains, losing himself
among beeches and deep blue. Then takes my hand again
and silently tells me the infinite paths of the sky.

from the Italian of Paolo Ottaviani

The Old Women of Magione

The old women of Magione hover round me like angels in the cramped confines of Orlando's minimarket, like lugubrious chrysalis angels who haven't yet learned to dance together on the tip of a needle or even fly;

heavy and lugubrious and awkward among the carelessly stacked shelves, they are sharp and sudden to take offence;

they haggle over prosciutto and won't let pass the slightest defect of merchandise, expect small discounts as a matter of course, an extra slice of pancetta;

they jump the queue in front of callow foreigners like me and chatter raucously like flocks of crows and are full of unbelievable tenderness.

The old women of Magione hover round me like angels with feet of lead, lifting their difficult arthritic limbs over unopened deliveries and torn cellophane,

while Orlando at the checkout counter ignores the growing queue and barks voluminous Italian into his cellular telephone.

And Orlando is full of the tenderness of old women, over the years he has become hermaphrodite from inhaling this atmosphere of suppressed love;

he cares for us with time-consuming fussiness, he wants us to buy the cheaper water, he'll change it although he has already rung up the dearer stuff on the till;

this develops into a diplomatic stand-off as the old women wait patiently behind me, racked with the growing pains of their wings.

The old women of Magione have survived war and peace, they have survived want and plenty, they have raised children and lived with emptiness;

they have nothing left but chatter which is the rattling of their old bones, and a deep well of tenderness hidden somewhere in the vast territories of their skulls;

they hover round me at a great distance in Orlando's small overcrowded shop, they care for me across light years of space;

they are my mother and father smiling over me as I woke one distant Christmas morning, they are my brothers and sisters from distant galaxies;

when I wake in the middle of the night I am soothed back to sleep by listening to the soft rustling of their wings.

And I am soothed back to sleep by a vision of a huge angel called Orlando arguing with God on a cellular telephone;

whose wings twitch with the twitchings of his face as he remonstrates with the silent divinity at the other side of the universe;

whose wings brush against carelessly piled tins of peeled plum tomatoes, against vacuum packs of espresso, against delicately balanced stacks of toothpaste, and merchandise comes crashing down behind him as he puts God in his place, calling him many colourful Italian names not intended to please;

as he sits there long after closing time with the curved blades of his pinions scraping the ceiling and feathers dusting the floor, pouring a torrent of angelic choler into the mouth-piece;

until it's midnight in Magione and there's a multitudinous rustling of old women's wings in the sky between the stars and the streetlights.

School Video

Conor sits at a desk with three other children, searching among spread cards for pictures to match the words on the easelled board behind him. Finding nothing to fit, at a loss, he appeals to Rosita, who is hoarding cards on her lap. She refuses to part with any, but Luca gives him one that turns out to be a dud. Conor stands up to protest: *Maestra! Maestra!* Graziella arrives huge and towering, a Roman-nosed prop forward who is really an angel in disguise, because there's an unfakeable atmosphere of happiness in this video given to us as a parting gift.

And yet I keep seeing adult faces on these childish heads, as if a defect in the film's capacity to capture light had somehow revealed the future. Especially here in this sequence, where the six boys are huddled together on a bench at the back of the classroom: I see in the strange light a giddy group of European politicians or partisans at a peace conference. Or perhaps it is the past that has been bared by this quirk of clairvoyance, the generations that went into the making of these features, and I am looking at a convocation of grinning tribal elders.

Conor is sitting in front of the class, reciting an episode from the story of Peter and the Wolf. Now he looks more like a girl than a boy, reminding me forcefully of my younger sister, his aunt. He loves being the centre of attention, his eyes dart around, they have messages for the eyes of the children in front of him. Finishing his piece, he rises and slaps the seat of the chair as an invitation to Luca, waiting in the corner, next in line. Luca recites sing-song, shyly tugging at the ends of his trousers, a sedentary acrobat.

Maria Grazia, who has spina bifida, sits in her wheelchair and rolls her tongue. Her eyes are bright and alert. Chiara, Conor's *femme fatale*, comes up and carresses her. They communicate: Maria Grazia rolls her tongue again and Chiara affectionately imitates her.

Maria Grazia sits among the other angels; she is the one with broken wings. And Graziella is the huge seraphim with layer upon layer of feathers, the watching nurturing presence. What will become of her fledglings, what will they make of their lives, where will they end? At least it is clear that in this classroom they were happy.

Afterwords

Love in November

(for Margaret)

Love in November is when phantoms wait
impatiently for me at home, but you
delay me in the wet
wind-buffeted streets outside
some suddenly sprouted garden shop
to look at plastic pots of thyme and parsley.

Love in November is when your car won't start
and you have me over the faulty barrel
of the ignition, take me away
from my novel to peer into the eyes
of archetypically wise
mechanics and measure our chances.

Love in November is a few words
thrown in the mouth of the wind
as we walk the streets together;
remembering what is so
like us in this, to throw
a few words at the wind and laugh.

Lime Trees

I stand in the somewhat battered plenitude
of my life, a man in his own garden
in the almost middle of May overawed
by the beauty of lime trees.
They form the boundary between two schools
on the other side of the wall,
these tall latecomers into leaf;
and how long have I waited until
the catch in my breath
when I stepped out the back door last night
and they glistened fresh as morning
in the pallor of city lights?
But gazing at them today
in the slightly drunk mid-afternoon,
I am baffled, ill at ease.
How can I hold my ground against this :
lime trees in newest leaf,
gentle arboreal fireworks
showering in stillness,
clusters of leaf-green stars?
Pendulous with their random constellations,
a receding row of universes,
they stand as much beyond
my language as beyond my wall,
and I'm afraid to look at them
much longer, in case I'll be struck dumb
or spend the rest of my days
gibbering about lime trees.

'You Parked Your Car In Fontamara'

(i.m. Ignazio Silone)

You parked your car in Fontamara,
when evening sunlight lapped the town
like water. And what else could you do
but drive until you reached the Fount
of Bitterness? We knew
by your faces as you passed
that one of us had left his mark.

I want to be buried under the bell
of the ancient church, a cross
upon my tomb, facing the place
where water once and no longer shines.
You had the look of water that doesn't count
for all its vital properties,
on your way to the Bitter Fount.

Water for all, that must
be drained because those without thirst,
who never knew drought, so planned.
Bury me under the bell of the ancient church,
facing the look of water on dry land.
We knew you by that look of absent water;
because you parked your car in Fontamara.

Pescina dei Marsi, 3 July 1997.

65

Mixed Salad

Parmesan of dandruff
on middle-aged lapels,
crows' nests accruing to tall trees
in spring, cosy cartels,

anniversaries, dead and alive,
the needle of the speedometer
rising to dispute
first in line with a juggernaut,

Zimbabwean batiks,
Pablo Neruda's metaphors,
good friends and charlatans,
Mad Cow Disease, Alzheimer's,

the fisherman's sad nets,
the sea's rustling girdle,
the parish pump supporters
in aquamarine Toyotas,

walking arm in arm
with my son after football
despite time's incubations,
every inflexible principle.